POWERTALK

Therése Halscheid

cover design
John Bratina

ACKNOWLEDGMENTS

Some of these poems first appeared in original or previous forms or are forthcoming in the following magazines and anthologies: *Coastal Forest Review, Creation Spirituality, Footwork: Paterson Literary Review, New Jersey Outdoors, Poems for the Wild Earth, The Schuylkill Valley Journal, Sedona: Journal of Emergence, Snowy Egret, Under a Gull's Wing, Verve, Wild Earth, Without Halos, Woman and Earth.*

This book is dedicated to God.

MAGIC WORD

when
i was too weak
        to
            ride
my bicycle
i repeated
        sounds
            in my name
until each
        spoke

turned as
        one
        moving wheel

CONTENTS

This is a book about sharing. Earth sharing with people, people sharing with the earth and it is also a tribute to those who provided house-sitting opportunities and to those who shared their homes with me so I could continue writing.

Although the book is arranged sequentially, pages are not numbered. This is because all earth experiences are equally important. It is also because Earth's way of sharing is unlimited, spontaneous and simultaneous. What you read has already occurred in some way, is happening while you read it, and will exist in your mind for future adventure.

You may choose to read front to back, but you may also create your own journey by bringing to each page your own perceptions while allowing the book to unfold. This method of reading is used by Eastern scholars to explore Chinese philosophical classics. Nonlinear reading suggests that by opening the book at random— through chance—readers select appropriate passages and can then contemplate meaningful coincidences between the printed words and their daily lives. Meaningful connections, known as synchronicity, bring heightened inner awareness to outer experiences. And, by applying the same printed message to varying life situations, many levels of understanding will occur. Poems and journal entries can transcend meaning over time.

The publication of this book has been supported by Val and Tom Bethell, Kathy and Joe Fugaro, Pamela and Stephen Interlanté, Ceil and Joe McFadden and Mary, my mother, for the sharing of their homes. To all, a special thanks.

PURPOSE

... as I was crying, I stopped suddenly and thought of trees and flowers and innocent scurrying animals. I said to myself, how good it would be to become like them—like trees swaying, standing tall in a woods somewhere. How beautiful they are, peaceful and pure.

I was filled with incredible longing and love for trees knowing they could be true friends and harmless. I was calmed, given knowledge they were suffering too.

I was being told they were suffering just as I was suffering and that's why I was here ... to help them. This is not my only purpose. But, as a human being among many, many other humans, I suddenly knew to assist the waters, air and the soil. I fully understood the plant, animal and stone life was wounded and we could take part in rejuvenating their existence. Helping the earth by opening our hearts and through our heart centers, Earth could help us heal.

I have been crying recently. At the pond, or when moonbeams and sunlight shine through the bedroom window and my eyelids flutter. How can a human wake crying? Yet, it is true.

This is not sadness. I am afraid of the love. Afraid of the power of Earth's intimacy entering. As colors brighten, as everywhere around me I see faces in stones. Feel bliss from the flowers and slowly understand what the red bird has been saying when I sit on the tar roof waiting for nightfall before hugging the pine.

I think about simplicity, about my purgation of material things and I think this: Although I may not feel it now—while I live in an apartment, while I still have antiques around me—when possessions are gone and I leave too, I shall fill in other ways. Through an internal way of being, I shall know richness.

It is like this. A pitcher is full of creamy milk which is delicious, and the white is lovely to look at. When milk is poured from the pitcher, when the pitcher is emptied of milk, it fills with air. Even in the process of emptying the pitcher, with each drop gone, each tiny space is replaced with oxygen. So the pitcher is still full. The pitcher is always full. Always.

The milk is material substance, the object I see. But a pitcher with air sustains since air is paramount for my existence. Through what appears to be nothing, I am given what is needed most. And so it shall happen, as these objects leave an inner invisible voice awakens for writing.

It is the same with wild flowers. In the beginning of my loving them, I would think nothing of picking buttercups or bouquets of purple violets. I would place them in jars with water and enjoy them until they wilted.

Now, I cannot take flowers from grasses any more than I could cut someone's toe. My mind receives them from a distance and their beauty is more striking. Flowers are my teachers. Fragrant teachers. And by daring to stand in meadows empty-handed, through absence, they enter my heart.

COLLECTION

By June, the antique dealers
had taken every old piece

out of the apartment
with large windows and white walls

carried them
across the tar roof, walked them

down a weathered flight of stairs
stacking them in trucks

roping them tight
before they drove off leaving

the faint smell of carved wood
in the wind, the smell

of oil lamps and hand painted plates
and everything else

I had learned how to buy
not by reading

not by reading by running
my hands through the grain

using the sense of touch to call up
the energy of the past

that sprung out of the wood
at night while I sat in the dark

red chair, resting my head back
in a field of mahogany flowers.

BLACKWOOD, NEW JERSEY

After I sold everything, she gave me rooms with white ceilings and walls, white rugs across floors. It is my job to guard them while she is gone, to rise from wood or plastic chairs watering the borrowed luminous flowers at the end of each day....

STORMS

I was standing
in the yard
when the mouth of sky opened

he was whispering at first
then slanting his words down
hard

                         into
                         my hands
                         stretched-out
                         coiled like a bowl.

I said nothing. In return
it was enough to watch wind
roughhousing with trees

to feel
the eyes of   all
the neighbors

                 glaring
behind windows
where they stayed

cool
and dry and
full of wonder why
I kept jumping off the quiet porch

for each storm
landing like its eye
centered and calm

untouched
by lightning—
on the lawn they never knew

heavy rains which healed
my troubled body
were   messages

from water beings
                 prying open
                 my palms.

OCEAN CITY, NEW JERSEY

I understand who I am by how I see. Today, as lemon light pointed down through a cloud, a beam warming the water. I am water too. Fluid, shimmering and flipping, a sparkling wave. I am white froth washing up, rainbows in mists, mists, sand, glistening sea stones and shells.

I am the color of peach touching my chest, healing myself as I walk out of day and enter my darkness, travel willingly through what I have chosen with hope glowing as a moon and the stars.

RECORD KEEPERS

I have come
to learn
from the wise
tales
to stand
where water moves
in waves

splashing
the right message
into the mind
bringing words
from the sea
stones tossed
to the surface

revealing
their forms
in the sand
glistening
and wet
as I skim over
the rose

the white
and marbled ones
reading
their thoughts
through my palms
as though each
were a page.

CONCH

it was saying
what has been
said in
drum-
beats   *the heart*
          hears

there are voices
between my left
and right ear
between the skull
and spine

echoes
of these
waves   *again*
         and again

they
have found

another hiding
place
    to do
       their singing.

CYCLES

When
I held
the moon shell
in my hand
it spoke
of a
day
when
I would
trace
its surface
when I would
be willing
to make small
concentric circles
with my eyes
focused
on the spiraling
path   the path
that leads
in
through
chambers
of this shell
and there
I would
review all
the lessons
of all my lives
being stored
like grains
of sand
blown
into
an endless
sheet
of see-through
glass

CLAM

It was the way

the gull came
to get it, first

a peck
then a pry, another

perch on its shell,
one soar

through air—
claws carrying

my white jewel
my own

legs in flight
running toward rocks

where it lie
already

cracked
and half opened—

it was
crying

and then not
crying that way

it happened that way.

LIFT

Once

I was surrounded by bayberry
and sea lavender, so hidden

in the sand dunes
not even the sun knew

where I was—
it could not follow

the unexpected
movements of arms

fingers reaching out
for the air turning

myself over, turning over
to trust

limbs
as they twirled away

from the earth,
spiraled up weightless

in total surrender to a wind dance
which ended

by spinning me down
in slow motion through trees.

It was difficult to get the story in my mind, on paper. I would write, then walk away from the computer making excuses. Then I would realize I was making excuses and go back to create. It went on like that, up and down, with me trying to stretch my idea into a story. It was about a swine farm, and I was discouraged because I couldn't convey what I had been thinking inside.

Then Jean came. We decided to sit in the kitchen and talk but I was still pondering the story while looking beyond the sliding glass door at the sky. It was nearing dusk and fabulous peach hues were spreading.

Jean didn't notice. Her chair wasn't facing the lagoon. She kept talking and I was listening but also watching the sunset as well as thinking about the story when a white cloud went by. In the shape of a pig! A pudgy white pig and I couldn't believe it. A pig with his head bent down, with his snout buried in another cloud as if he were eating slop.

I wanted to shout out, say, "Turn around, Jean! Turn around!"

But I was embarrassed. It was unspeakable to be thinking of swine the same time the sky had a pig cloud floating by.

CLOUD FIGURES

for hours
the gray animals

have been stampeding
out of the black
forest

in
the sky—

shape shifting
as they leap off the cliff
of the world

and onto a trail of pink
wind which leads
to the sun

so
they
can graze freely

in its yellow field—
and leave

the loud
shots of the thunder-
beings

behind.

KILLING TIME

The beach is empty in autumn
and all along the boardwalk

shops are closing one by one
with barricades

with signs: GOING OUT FOR MORE
BUSINESS, BUY NOW!   I stop,

eat pizza by the slice then move on
into an arcade

where electric games cave in
around me, sucking me

onto airstrips and racetracks
the battlefields, the loud sounds

of guns shooting
are in the distance, coming closer

and I am lost.   No,
I am only entering a world

I am not used to—
missing the flowers in the forest

missing the forest—
I place a sweaty hand

on the palm reading machine
which does not work

does not need to work
I know how to use the quarter it takes

to fly away on the pink horse
with the white pretty mane.

CONTROL

a woman
stands by the sea selling
a handful of kites, even after summer

she continues the job—
through winter she paces
across shells

washed up
and along the shoreline
you can follow her silhouette

the weathered hands holding
strings, holding diamonds set
in the sky

on the beach
she does not worry,
when they do not sell

she thinks of gusts, of winds to come,
which kite might take her
through the air, lift her

out of earth's illusions, above sands
she believes she is running on, not real-
izing

she can fly now
if she wants to by just letting go

DISRUPTION

By midnight, the water had risen
all around the sea houses

submerged
the wood docks, splashed over

the bottom decks
hiding white lawns with smooth stones

and shell gardens,

hiding the fear of those of us
who stayed, trapped

by waves breaking
beneath the flickering lamps—

it was too late

to push the wet car over
the sopping bridge, it was too late

to save the finned ones tossed
from the sea

slapping their gills
against the exhausted earth

when the tide pulled back,
and the small town rose crying

to wring itself out
as everything stilled.

SECOND HEAVEN

It was important to walk
on water to stand
firm on deck

when the seven colors
of dusk rushed by

to face
the parting
of day through waves

rolling each color out
one after the other over
the rim of the sea

I sailed
to find

the rim of the sea
I followed night—

anchored

where stars could reflect
what was hidden
beyond

a dark fluid sky
to jump
into

... *throughout the Pine Barrens, tree faces were revealing themselves so I would trust. So I would connect with the consciousness of the forest by watching expressions. So I would learn through what I knew as seriousness and through what I knew as smiling.*

Though, this was not necessary. It is not necessary to see faces on trees to understand what they are saying. Trees know this. But these woods also knew I needed a way to relearn.

I say relearn because I remember tree talking as a child but called it pretending.

Today, they were proving "more than play." There was too much power here, there was wisdom being offered beyond what I could have created.

The lesson was on giving. The lesson was how to become brave to receive.

ANIMAL SELF

It is almost dusk when I turn
down the dirt road
to be with trees

to enter the sanctuary
in the woods where no one goes—
where I can dance

without clothes
without being conscious
of my skin or worried

about red scars and the dark marks
just allowing the shy
organ to fall

freely
against the rugged flesh of trees
limbs finding limbs

finding arms coiled like green-
brier slow
dancing

from trunk to trunk—
until the body loses its shame.

TWILIGHT

it is important

> *to reach the forest before night*
> *falls in the woods*

> *to stand*
> *where stretched out shadows of trees*

> *drape around*
> *the rim of the earth*

> *and where I can dance*
> *with my own form*

> *sprawled out*
> *to notice*

> *where animals are hiding*
> *by their distorted silhouettes,*

> *the flowers, all of us spreading*
> *the dark part of ourselves thin*

> *over the curved dirt, overlapping*
> *until not even the mind*

> *of the forest can distinguish*
> *our shapes—*

> *until animals' eyes*
> *turn into stars*

> *and my side of the world*
> *begins*

> *spinning*
> *its own mysterious black hole*

to walk through

I was standing in a yellow field sending joy into milkweed and red speckled bugs which were scurrying all over the pods when I heard it— the click of a gun. I turned. Two hunters were walking out of the woods, entering the meadow.

I remembered being cautioned about hunters perceiving motion as deer—like seeing a mirage when you are thirsty—and that, at times, they shoot at movements. Now I was afraid.

In panic, I screamed, "I'm not a deer, don't shoot! Don't shoot!" And one of them laughed.

"Deer don't wear red coats," the one who laughed shouted.

As soon as that happened, a big bubbly chuckle from the mind of the forest went into my mind. It wanted me to know it had been entertained.

TOTEM IN THE WOODS

To enter the thicket, to sleep
in the fairies' den
my body turns

into the fawn I have
seen in daydreams during
the night

dreams—
this is an animal
hiding inside my Self

coming out
to breathe the sweet air
bedding down

on the forest's
floor where birds
and scurrying beetles

even squirrels
are not afraid
when I extend my hooves

as if
I had four arms
to gather them all

against my coat,
rest that way
until it is time to walk back

into human form.

ENERGY FIELD

When I learned that humans
were living rainbows

with funnel shaped lights,
that they had seven

colors lined up and spinning
from the base

of the spine
to the crown of the skull—

I ran through woods
as a beaming vessel shooting

love into trees, colorful
love onto birds on

through the fawn in the thicket
until the entire forest fell

in a trance
and began its own healing

from the liquid white
spraying out of my head—

from the violet ray
of the mind and of the heart

with its green arrow
aimed

at the moss of the earth
curing the wild

flowers one by one
as the meadow grew—

gave back
a gift for my eyes

more brilliant color than these.

RHYDYCROESAU, ENGLAND

I see them in the morning, watch them from my window. Tom picking the raspberries. Val and the pony.

This is the place of giant blooms and singing birds. Roses, lavender, heather, honeysuckle and pansies. Owls, thrushes, blue and marsh tits. Even the natural spring at the top of the hill has found a way down, into their cottage. All day everything will bend, fly and flow towards them.

They will not speak of it this way. They never mention themselves.

TAN Y GRAIG UCHAF
Welsh, "Highest Under the Rock"

I remember reading the sign
Tan y Graig Uchaf
wondering what it meant
as we drove
the narrow dirt road
to your English cottage
parked the car
next to the three hundred
year old white cottage built
into the side of the hill

a home high up
overlooking the grayish blue
green hills of Wales,
their colors struggling
to blend with the sky

as you carried
my earth tone suitcase
up a flight of wooden stairs
explaining
the meaning of the name
while you walked—
speaking of the rock
the summit where water flows
from the rock, trickles down
to the pond where shubunkins
are swimming in circles

into a small sink
in the room where I stayed
gazing
out a window
the size of an entire wall

the night
a wild storm spoke
and I knew
but did not know how
I knew the language of the sky
rolling out its message
in tongues, using bright talk
to light up what was shuddering
beneath us the valleys
with slanted flowers, glowing black
and white sheep.

SUN AND MOON AT THE SAME TIME

The sun was bright orange
before setting
behind two distant peaks,
in front of the light blue sky,
as we began our walk
around a racetrack
overgrown with high weeds
and foxglove—
a path barely visible
but still circling the top of the hill
where horses galloped
a hundred years before this year now
overturning earth with their hooves
kicking up rocks, the dust blasting
out of the hill a century of the same
dust stirred up
settling back down

as we rounded the bend
a full moon was rising

sending silver beams
through apparitions of Victorian men,
through gold fobs dangling from pockets,
and there were women
with long see-through skirts
puffed out, blowing
in the wind
we saw a few of the bronze age workers
leaving huts
to make night fires and rugged tools—
all of them
stepping out
from what we see as past
onto a present course

around the track where no one wins
here, there are only revolutions

with a sun and a moon shining
at the same time
on this human
race.

HARDY, ARKANSAS

I decided to sleep in the hammock house and it seemed as if I was awake the entire night listening to sounds: a brook gurgling over rocks, katydids and cicadas. It was like an orchestra and bullfrogs all around the rim of the pond were the percussion.

I kept swaying, cradling myself almost the whole night, feeling rhythms, trying to figure out how creatures and water and rocks knew how to blend sounds together—how I could fit in. What would be my wild sound if I allowed myself to make it?

It was interesting but I was also nervous. About ticks and snakes, about bears wanting to grab—but nothing like that ever happened. Before dawn there were crows: *Caw caw caw! Caw caw caw! Caw to the world and tell them what we're saying!*

In the excitement, I tipped the hammock and startled some deer. They were grazing nearby and when they sensed the fumbling they leaped over tree stumps into the forest.

It was then that I decided to walk back to the motor home where I was staying and wish for their return. I made an inward wish which spread outward and then upward into the sky.

When they came, Mother with two speckled fawns, they were most graceful. Peacefully eating leaves.

This morning Joe took Kathy to a far away dentist. She has a toothache and not long after they left, I sat outside. I was journaling, sitting in a white chair leaning over a round table with hummingbirds, cherry tomatoes and potted impatiens to my right and the left. With sun sparkling through trees, with a breeze which kept tickling my skin all over at once and it was also laughing when, all of a sudden, I looked up wanting my body to blend with the earth. To become one with the foothill as I had done with the sea.

I stood, walked naked into the brown grass between the motor home and the pond, and began learning about myself by watching my shadow. And found loveliness there, in shapes and slow movements, in wild hair flapping against the curve of my spine. Unruly hair celebrating its freedom to curl every which way because I had not combed it. I had not yet braided or twisted it into a bun.

Limbs bending, fingers feathered through air unfolding, I circled the pond pirouetting past frogs and then twirled into the woods, nymph-like, light-footed, toes barely touching the dirt between trees.

I was learning something beyond body by not wearing garments. It felt pretty, but not people pretty. It was different. The soil was a mirror reflecting the way Earth sees me inside.

DANCING OUT OF THE FLESH

There were only five houses
scattered far apart on top
of the hill,
and on certain days
there were no family members
in four of the houses,
and there were other days
when four houses on the hilltop
were empty
and you left home, too

shopping
in towns miles from the mountains

while I stayed behind
unbuttoning my shirt
for the earth
unzipping my pants—
the cloth
falling away from my skin
onto the dirt road
as soon as the red
color of your car
disappeared in the bright orange dust

the cloth bunched, left
fluttering like an autumn leaf pile

as I brushed the trunk
of my body
against boulders and trees,
bending limbs forward
and back
while shadows dimmed
from the brilliant white
soul shape
dancing out of the flesh—
extending

extending through the dark forest
as wild animals stilled.

MASSAGE IN THE OZARK MOUNTAINS

In the hammock house,
in the woods

at the bottom of the hill,
near where the brook trickles

over ancient rocks,
near the constant babbling

babbling sound of a brook,
there is a silent you and me

and you dipping hands
in a bowl of scented oils.

My eyes are shut.

But I see you,
your fingers lifting out

of the bowl,
glowing from the sun

shining in
through the screen—

the oil
spread all the way down

the length
of my pebbled spine

the same way water rubs stone—
your hands

polish the surface
of the flesh, soothing bones

while blood flows
as a fresh mountain stream.

FLOATING DOWN SPRING RIVER
Mammoth Spring, Arkansas

When we dipped our feet
in water the color of green
glass, the shade of old bottles,
the river opened to reveal
the rock bed beneath us,
the shape of the stones
still slowly being polished
by liquid bubbling up
out of pores
flowing over the curved surface
of the planet carved
by this road the water was making.

We eased down in tubes
tossed our heads back
flopping limbs
over the black rubber sides
and laughed
at the whirling shapes—
the way movements
made concentric ripples
which splashed against smaller ripples
made by trout and turtles
popping out of the current briefly
before diving back down.

Along the bank cones of light
darted from centers of flowers
I caught this spinning
by squinting my eyes,
watched how brightness
funneled out touching
all ripples overlapping
until, like gears in a timepiece,
all that swirled upon the river
and the river
spiraled out of separation—
merged into one round ticking design.

HADDONFIELD, NEW JERSEY

I am sleeping in the attic, in the room where I slept as a child. No bed. No bed now, just lying on the floor rolling wherever stars spotlight the rug.

I am learning how to appreciate, through sky bolts and swaying tops of trees. By feeling sweet high winds as they blow through the small east window. Teaching. Up here, the high winds are always teaching exactly what I need to learn.

As a child, yes, and now there are lessons about everything around me being perfect.

When it does not seem this way—they say I am not seeing.

GIFT

A feather falls

>*in the grass.*
>*There are no birds flying by*
>*there are no sounds of crows*
>*or jays*
>
>*in the air I cannot find the sun—*
>*only a sudden gust of blue*
>*wind pulling me out the screen*
>
>*door, out of the abandoned*
>*porch*

where I write

>*there is a garden*
>*that grows nothing*
>
>*but*
>*Faith*
>*between*
>
>*the soil and sky, I can feel it*
>*when I write I can catch it*
>*hiding in the high weeds*
>*after turning myself*
>
>*over to trust*
>*like the feather*
>*falling without the bird today, just*
>
>*lying down*
>*detached.*

WALKING STICK
in memory of Dan Iacovino

Walking back
through the garden where nothing grows

where nothing grows, a brown patch marks
the exact spot

the old man whittled.
I can see the knife he carved with

pointed down in a circle of dry grass,
I can find it by watching silver

reflected on the underside of leaves
beneath the tree where I lay, faceup,

with his walking stick beside me.
I am eyeing the empty garden

observing two lopsided stone ovens
with iron grills

where his small body
bent over the wood and the blade

where elastic suspenders crisscrossed
across his back as he moved

the knife back and forth smoothing a branch
with shavings falling down around him

birds swooping
to gather them up quickly

after he had gone. After he had gone,
I still recalled

the cold Christmas morning
when I was a child knocking on his door

how he handed me
a walking stick which took one autumn

season to carve, how his lips curled
upward the same moment

my fingers folded over the top of the cane
grasped the head of the bleeding

Jesus—he kept repeating
the staff would be useful someday

as my hand closed
to open up to receive the piercing splinters

from the crude bark he left natural as a crown.

... I did walk by the pond. And while I walked I sent love to nature until colors and scents heightened, until my beingness blended with every other being and I was awash with joy.

Where a tree had been struck by lightning and lie half in, half out of the water, I cried. I could feel it dying, and also the slow death of a wise feeble one nearby. The body of the wise one was mostly hollow and had an entrance like a cave. Never having entered a tree except through my mind, I crawled in and then stood upright inside it.

I remained hidden for a long time, projecting silent messages to live to live to live!

LESSONS
for Lyuba

In daydreams I say to her

take us back to the mountain
where birds store colors

for dawn
I say we are young

but must think
like old mountains

think of new ways
to stand—

where the logger swings his ax
our flesh should have syrup

where the miner takes gold
we must flower

as thistles
and meadowsweet—

we will find the spot
where uncombed hair

is still the strongest thicket,
where hearts are winter berries

despite the frozen vine.

FIREBUG

Your soul b u r s t
in front of me
                              yellow
everywhere
I run I stand
as one skin statue
                              silent
between
the foot of this tree
and the mouth of that

stone
only

my hair blowing
my long hair flashes
of curly lightning—

          when you are   yellow
I am   still
posing

in the
exact middle
of a large black night

          your god
          comes out   comes
                           into me.

BLACKOUT

In a town
next to the one I grew up in
a blind boy who does not speak
positions his skateboard
on the sidewalk
places one foot on its neon surface
and uses his other
to push off into the night.
I am observing
from a distance, startled
by the sudden excitement
of trees
gold leaves creaking
on their stark, black limbs
as he races by
zooming up then down
each neighbor's drive
concrete crumbling
under the weight of his wheels
as he gathers speed as he skates
off cement curb cliffs
loosening the tar hard streets
while he turns, the street
lamps
bending
in half over houses
from wind he makes with his arms,
crashing through roofs
caving in rooms
where families are transfixed
to blaring, blue screens—
it is the only way
he knows how
to shock them into silence
to rush them out
into the dark
singing grasses
and hear the way he hears
earthtalk
without using their eyes.

DELPHINIUM

Each week the woman
everyone
in the old town
ignores
enters the floral shop,
reaches
into the black bucket
her long fingers
almost touching the still water
and pulls up a stem growing
at least twenty buds.

She raises the tip
of the branching herb
to her ear,
listens
for tunes growing
in groups of five
petals ready
to unravel themselves
into loud, purpling horns.

"I like flowers
with sounds coming
from fuzzy, yellow centers,"
she says handing
the florist a one dollar bill
then hobbles away
kindly understanding
he does not yet
understand her kind

those who buy them
for their faint notes
bursting
into concert—
like wind instruments
blowing sweet music
through the bedroom air
the moment sun strikes
each one open
to wake them at dawn.

THE TENTED WILLOW

The air is solid black
yet I sense a tree swaying
on the other side of the river
the same way I spotted
campsites far away
when I was young, to see
the place of making fires
before my father's car brought it
into view

and there is something
I already know
about this willow
staked by the water
which makes this scene familiar
without my touching it, which makes it easy
to shrink my body

returning limbs to their child size
reliving shortened
autumn days
when I talked without speaking
to this kind of tree
sending a thought form
into the wood, feeling it spread
all the way down the length of the bark—
it is so

it is another way
of listening to earth's language
posing a question
where there is always an answer
gliding
in the river
drawn up through the roots.

RAIN AND I

After it stopped
I stood
on the river bank
watching
an opposite current
slowly pull together
what the storm
had driven downstream,
the reflected features
of my face—
the image
winds and rain
had rearranged,
the furious waves
of hair rippled out
now quietly twined
back in a braid
and through its coming,
my coming together
through stillness—
I noticed raindrops
which had been clinging
to the maple
above me, falling
away from the tree
splashing like tears
hurrying
to return
to their floating eyes
while the last
of the autumn
leaves
spiraled down, too,
landing
inside an oval mouth
opened
as a whirlpool,
swallowing
each of the gold shapes
quickly—
filling myself
with light.

IMPROVISATION

I only wanted to hear waves
like bedsheets clipped
to the thin line of the horizon
flapping themselves out—
their bleached corners
almost touching
the back of the station wagon
where I lay, covered,
floating in a dream
moments before an officer
shone his lights
through the fogged up windows

when my instincts awakened
and quickly flattened
my body down, the color
of my hair turning
the same color as the blankets
like the startled rabbit I saw
earlier, his fur blending in
with the dunes. I am still
as the squirrel,

"Just another animal
sleeping under stars!"
I want to shout out
but know to be silent, know how
to be unnoticed until he leaves
and even then it takes time
for my hands to want to reach out
for the wheel, to toss a coin
in the tollbooth's wire basket
and watch it fall like a moon
sadly dropping
behind the rim of the sea

I keep repeating, "No one takes away
what we are meant to enjoy,"
and listen to a cassette
of ocean music playing
as I move off the island
the jar of quarters beside me
glowing
like small silver full moons
themselves.

EARTH INSIDE ME

It happens in daydreams, and there are night dreams where I find myself in lands never found in waking states.

These are places where everything speaks. These are places where I can fly or sit upon moss covered rocks gazing into the bright glassy eyes of honest animals and know instantly what I have done right, where I have gone wrong, and what can still be created in the world that I perceive with opened eyes.

JUST ONCE TO BE A ROCK

It must have been
shortly after midnight
when I saw myself rising
from the bed
leaving my skin
my hair trailing
the length of the pillow—
I was a twin of the one
sleeping

traveling through woods, searching
for the place where bluebells
and bleeding hearts are bent
over rocks, the garden
where ivy glows from a moon
and stars shining
through limbs of the trees

all I wanted
was to rest with the stones,
to huddle with fingers like vine
tendrils coiled around feet
pressing heels
in the earth
keeping my face hidden
between slightly parted
knees

all I wanted
was one night of being rubbed
like a stone
by the gardener
who does not judge what is felt
when he comes moving his quiet hands
back and forth

reading
symbols carved
on the mineral kingdom, the curved
ribs and long line
of my spine releasing what I am,
earthly records of lives
I have lived—
the spirit tempered
inside my solid, rock body.

FRAMED FACE

They call it sleep.
And all night
I was doing this, sleeping
in an attic
head pressed
against a small
window screen,
moonlight checkered
across my chest
the rhythm of my breath
slowed down
each time I entered
the dream, the scenario
repeating itself
in the dark—
eyes rolling
behind eyelids
watching the same image
flashback
through the mind

the place of faces

hidden in black water,
limbs anchored
at the bottom of a pond—
only the worried expression
of who I am
was struggling to surface
every time the dream came
each time my face
had risen more—
bubbling up blurred
with long curly strands
of hair floating
on top, coiled
like rope twined
about nothing
yet pulling me upward
until I was clearly
smiling
through a buoyant circle
of bright autumn leaves.

MIRAGE

At night I follow dreams
into a desert willing to share

secrets about itself. I move in
through the chaparral, eyeing

the lava mountain
it wants me to climb, to hear whispers

from the coarse, black rock
of knowing

which first came out of the earth
in liquid flame—

that cooled and piled wisdom high
upon the land

where I sleep/walk
to reach the peak of hidden knowledge

of the mind traveling
under folds of a white blanket

rippled—
like dunes of endless grains of sand.

MOSAIC

Walking, slow walking
graceful

sometimes olde
sometimes young

but always in   long
dresses from   long ago

a blurred little boy
beside me.

In front, the woods
where I enter alone

always through my Self
letting my long hair wave

a long ribbon laugh
out loud.

In the leaves
a smooth rock hides, but seeks

the same cool
pool of water

I wade in,
dragging my hand inside

the liquid rising
its clearness

splashing up
for colour, my breasts.

KNOWING TREE
In a dream
a tree
knew about me.
He took sorrow
into his roots, he took
joy up then down
like sap, my life
flowed through Tree
and through this tree
secrets grew
like hidden rings
expanding inside
his trunk.
You could read
me
that way
you could find me

in the dream

there was water,
moving, she was gently
slapping
against the tree.
She was learning
of my life
each time
she touched
she healed
roots aching
with knowledge
there were waves
washing
all sadness, all joy
out of Tree—

as if he
had been crying
to be cut down, as if I
       had become
           too much
              to bear.

GODSELVES

Everything was God
in the dream.
Trees were God.
Man
and womankind.
Rocks—
animals were God
and all species
could remain
God illuminated
breathing
in oval white cocoons
with the word God
imprinted
in brilliant letters
across white oval cocoons
as long
as we did not doubt
our Godselves
or create
in judgment of others—
the way humans
have carried on
for years
making names
for ourselves,
clothes
for bodies
to hide their belief
in separate forms.

BRIGANTINE, NEW JERSEY

I woke early and recorded a dream about a man who wouldn't write about the sea. He did it this way. He would listen, and water had words. The same words, over and over. I don't remember what they were, but I knew I heard them. I saw them too. Like little thought forms, like small luminous clouds, iridescent bubbles rising out of the waves coming toward him.

And every day he would sit in the sand or sit on a rock jetty, way way out on the last rock waiting for sea words to come into his mind. Which was the opposite of what I thought was supposed to happen.

I thought humans chose words to write about sea.